The Barking Family Adventure Books

The Barking Family Halloween Adventure

I0172356

Written by

Amanda Welch

Illustrated by

Amanda Welch

The Grown-Up Stuff

Diamond, Ista, and Indi were three energetic and mischievous husky puppies who lived with the Barking family. Their owners, Mr. and Mrs. Barking, adored them and always made sure they had plenty of toys and treats to play with.

The puppies' favourite pastime was going

on adventures with the Barking twins,

Liam and Lucy.

Liam and Lucy were inseparable and shared a love for exploration, just like their furry friends. The four of them would go on long walks through the woods, and sometimes even sneak into the neighbour's garden to play with their cat, Whiskers.

But with Halloween just around the corner, the puppies and twins were determined to do something special to celebrate the spooky holiday.

As the leaves changed colour the puppies and twins brainstormed ideas for their Halloween adventure. They wanted something scary and exciting, but also safe for puppies and young children.

After much deliberation, Lucy came up with a brilliant idea. She suggested they have a Halloween-themed scavenger hunt in the woods near their house.

The other three were immediately on board, and the preparations began. The twins made a list of Halloween-themed items for the scavenger hunt, such as a pumpkin, a broomstick, and an old witch's hat.

Diamond, Ista, and Indi helped by gathering branches, leaves, and other natural materials to create a spooky atmosphere in the woods.

Finally, the day of the scavenger hunt arrived, and the puppies and twins were buzzing with excitement. Mrs. Barking helped decorate their bags with sharpie drawings of ghosts and spiders, and Mr. Barking gave them all flashlights and walkie-talkies for safety.

The group set off into the woods,

following the clues that Lucy had

carefully hidden along the way.

With each clue they found, the

puppies and twins grew more excited.

They discovered a pumpkin hidden

inside a hollow tree trunk, a

broomstick dangling from a branch,

and an old witch's hat perched on a

rock.

As they reached the final clue, they were met with a surprise. The last item on the list was a real-life witch, who turned out to be Mrs. Barking, dressed up in a spooky costume.

The puppies and twins howled with laughter as they realized it was just a prank, and they all enjoyed a delicious Halloween-themed picnic in the woods.

As the sun began to set and the moon rose high in the sky, Diamond, Ista, and Indi couldn't have been happier. They had gone on a thrilling adventure with their best friends and celebrated Halloween in a unique and unforgettable way.

From that day on, the puppies and

twins made it a tradition to have a

Halloween scavenger hunt every year.

And while they had many more exciting adventures together, this one always held a special place in their hearts.

For Diamond, Ista, and Indi, there was no better way to spend Halloween than with their beloved family and friends, searching for spooky clues and making wonderful memories that would last them a lifetime.

It was now time for Liam and Lucy and the puppy's to go to bed. They said goodnight and of to bed they went.

www.ingramcontent.com/pod-product-compliance
Lightning Source LLC
Chambersburg PA
CBHW041809040426
42449CB00001B/23